Images of
Burnley

Burnley Express

Images of
Burnley

The Breedon Books
Publishing Company
Derby

First published in Great Britain by
The Breedon Books Publishing Company Limited
Breedon House, 44 Friar Gate, Derby, DE1 1DA.
1996

Acknowledgement
To the staff of
Burnley Reference and Local History Library.

ISBN 1 85983 051 X

Printed and bound by Butler & Tanner Ltd., Selwood Printing
Works, Caxton Road, Frome, Somerset.

Colour separations by Colour Services, Wigston, Leicester.

Jackets printed by Lawrence-Allen, Weston-Super-Mare, Avon.

Contents

Introduction

THE history of Burnley stretches back (depending upon how far you want to go) to the days more than 800 years ago when it was little more than a cluster of homes round its ancient parish church of St Peter by the River Brun. It received its market charter just over 700 years ago – since when a lot has happened!

Suffice to say, leaping a few centuries and coming more up to date, the town became enveloped by the industrial revolution.

It saw the coming of the canal and the railway, the displacement of the handloom weavers, and the growth of factory-centred employment; until Burnley became the town reputedly with the greatest concentration of power looms in the world. King Cotton had been enthroned, though it was to be an industry both loved and hated by the increasing population which lived in mean streets surrounding the mills and toiled in warehouse and shed from early morning (with a break for breakfast and lunch) until the teatime whistle blew.

Those were the days of clogs and shawls, the knocker-up, gaslight and half-timers – youngsters who, when they were old enough, spent half their day in school and the rest in the mill. The industry continued with its slumps and booms until the early 1960s when swift decline set in, thanks to cheap imports (some of them woven on exported Lancashire looms).

In the meantime, the war had brought in firms escaping the blitz on the nation's major cities. Among them came Lucas, where pioneering work was done on parts of Sir Frank Whittle's jet engine. Other engineering firms – Platers and Stampers, Burnley Aircraft Products, Butterworth and Dickinson, to name a few – played their part in the war effort.

To add to engineering after the war, came Mullard, Michelin and Belling, mining was still going strong, and the railways were also still playing an active role. In the early 1960s, it was boom time, with the town's football club winning the League Championship, playing in Europe and reaching an FA Cup Final, with many big city clubs envying its results and apparently never-ending stream of youthful talent.

Then followed the decline of textiles and mining, and the railway. The town fought hard to bring in new jobs, civic leaders dangling the bait of empty factories and a loyal and hard-working labour force to prospective incoming industrialists – and although self-help and reliance have softened the decline, the impetus of those heady days has not quite been restored.

But there has been new industry and enterprise, and the pride of Burnleyites has not been dimmed. This book of pictures features much of the past, but there is also a quiet confidence in the future.

Peter Dankin

The Town Centre

An early impression of Burnley town centre with the 'gaumless' lamp in the centre, the Bull Hotel at the bottom of Manchester Road (left) and the premises of Cowgill & Smith (right), a firm of builders' merchants which remained under that name right up to recent years.

A crowded St James's Street – the year unknown.

Church Street, then so narrow it was only able to accommodate a single tram track.

Church Street in 1903, looking towards the centre and the Town Hall beyond.

Looking down St James's Street to the white Burton's building, site of the old Bull Hotel, and on towards the chimneys of the Weavers' Triangle.

Days of the steam trams before the turn of the century, with the Bull Hotel on the left and the Thorn Hotel on the right.

A busy St James's Street scene with steam trams having given way to electric tramcars.

Further along St James's Street, still in the horse and cart era.

Into the motor car age, and ready for a big change as 1960s demolition and rebuilding of the central area begins behind hoardings on the right.

Back to steam trams, but looking down St James's Street in the opposite direction.

Munn's corner in St James's Street.

A little later, but in days of the electric trams.

And again in the days when buses had replaced the trams

On the left of the street were the BSK café and the Palace Theatre, roughly on the site of the present Woolworth store.

Old buildings survive on the left and right of the picture taken before pedestrianisation of the town centre with the Keirby Hotel (here sporting the name of the Crest Motel) at the far end of the street.

Empty property, with Chancery Street on the right, as demolition of the market area was beginning in the 1960s.

Back of St James's Street with a view along the River Calder towards Clock Tower Mill, a prominent landmark in the 'Weavers' Triangle' which had to be partially demolished after the mill caught fire. The building still awaits a decision on its future.

The bottom end of St James's Street leading up to Westgate.

Westgate at its junction with Accrington and Padiham Roads.

Yorkshire Street in 1959-60 with scaffolding still up on the right of the newly-built Keirby Hotel.

The old three-arched Leeds and Liverpool Canal culvert in Yorkshire Street.

The archway is demolished as a new structure bears the canal water over the street.

The Hammerton Street Co-operative building for which the memorial stone was laid by Thomas Hughes, author of *Tom Brown's Schooldays*, in 1885 with the 'tower' prominent in this view from Hargreaves Street before the town's main Post Office replaced the building on the right.

The new bus station is seen in the background as work on the Centenary Way flyover goes ahead in the foreground.

Looking up Manchester Road from street level to the Town Hall.

And Manchester Road from a lofty perspective.

The Manchester Road corner with Red Lion Street changed from a butcher's shop (bottom picture) to the Savoy Cinema and Café, and then to the Martin's Bank building (top), which became Barclay's and is presently a retail store.

Inset is the Grimshaw Street entrance to what was the former Burnley Building Society headquarters, seen with the premises it replaced. The building society premises are now Borough Council offices.

A view over the centre of the town in its cotton heyday, probably from Clock Tower Mill, with Westgate visible in the foreground and the railway viaduct on the left.

This view extends from the police station and library to St Peter's Church and Burnley College, with Burnley General Hospital buildings in the distance.

People and Places

Burnley Football and Cricket Clubs' bag carrier Mr J.W.Needham.

Burnley has had its fair share of real characters, but they don't make 'em any more like this: J.R.'Catty' Rushton.

Above: These Russian cannons, souvenirs of the Crimean War, were a familiar landmark at the junction of Colne Road and Bank Parade. Sadly, the campaign to commandeer anything with scrap metal potential claimed them among its victims during World War Two and they were melted down.

Left: 'The British working man', Jimmy Pudding – whose waistcoat and jacket appear to have absorbed large portions of many of the puddings he may have eaten!

W. Vernon's hairdressing establishment at 25 Finsley Gate seems to have been a popular one, if the queue outside is anything to go by.

A good turnout of residents for the camera in Padiham Road.

This scene was also in Padiham Road at Cheapside, facing towards Burnley with All Saints' Church, Habergham, on the left.

Thorney Bank residents, in the Trafalgar Street area, gather in force, despite the wet day.

The canal warehouse can be made out through the gloom of this view along Mount Pleasant.

This was the outlook in John Street, off Calder Street, many years ago.

New homes arise in Ormerod Road, while the old Talbot and Sparrow Hawk Hotels remain standing.

Padiham Road swings round the corner at Gannow Top, with Boat Horse Lane on the right – long before the M65 was preceded by widescale demolition and a transformation of the area.

A busy lunchtime scene at the junction of Branch Road and Parliament Street.

Down Coal Clough Lane into the murk of the industrial town.

A wet day in Mills Street.

And it's not much brighter on the day of this picture in Fleet Street.

Lowerhouse Lane at the time it was boasting a new canal bridge.

The advertising hoardings were a familiar sight on Manchester Road in this pre-1965 picture.

And just around the corner in Manchester Road, looking down into town about the same time.

Looking up Westgate towards the Mitre with the tower of Holy Trinity Church above the rooftops.

Another busy route in and out of town these days, Briercliffe Road at the Casterton and Eastern Avenues roundabout.

Slum clearance was a big issue in immediate pre and postwar days, this being the scene in Healey Wood Road.

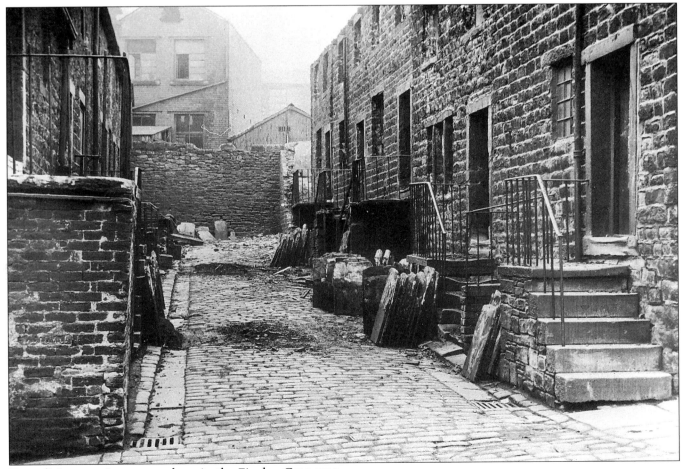

Demolition was in progress here in the Finsley Gate area.

But rebuilding was also in progress, viewed in this case by a civic party on the left.

And work here was in progress on the building of Lockyer Avenue.

The Trafalgar Street area was under the demolition contractor's hammer here.

And work was soon in progress on the construction of the ill-fated Trafalgar Gardens flats.

Trafalgar Flats began life as being a much trumpeted answer to the Corporation's housing problem but, in common with 1960s planning experiments in many parts of the country, failed to establish a true community spirit, soon deteriorated and, in this case, ended in a new clearance and 1990s redevelopment project – hopefully with the grim lessons of the past having been learned.

One success of the 1960s, however, was the Centenary Way flyover link road, with work on it here spanning the Leeds and Liverpool Canal.

And one street still left with plenty of pride was Palatine Square, where a residents' group got together to conserve its uniqueness.

Work on the link road which leads from the end of Padiham bypass to the M65.

One of the buildings which fell victim to motorway construction was St Mary Magdalene's, which had one of the most beautiful interiors of any church in the town, and its loss, shortly after this picture was taken, was mourned by many – despite its replacement by two new buildings, St Teresa's at Gannow and St Mary Magdalene's in Gawthorpe Road.

This was St Peter's Parish Church, hub of the early town, pictured in the days long before the churchyard tidy-up scheme which attracted a royal visit in 1966.

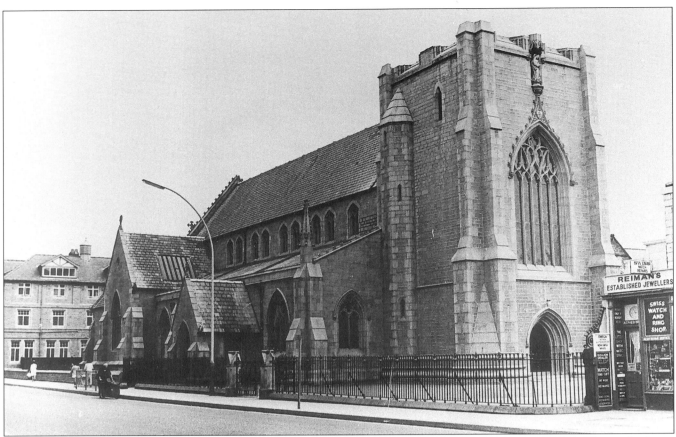

The largest Roman Catholic Church and parish in the town, St Mary's, Yorkshire Street, seen in 1974. Picture by Lynn Millard.

Wesley Church stood in Hargreaves Street, being demolished to make way for the present Central Methodist Church on the same site, which also included members from the demolished Brunswick Church in Manchester Road.

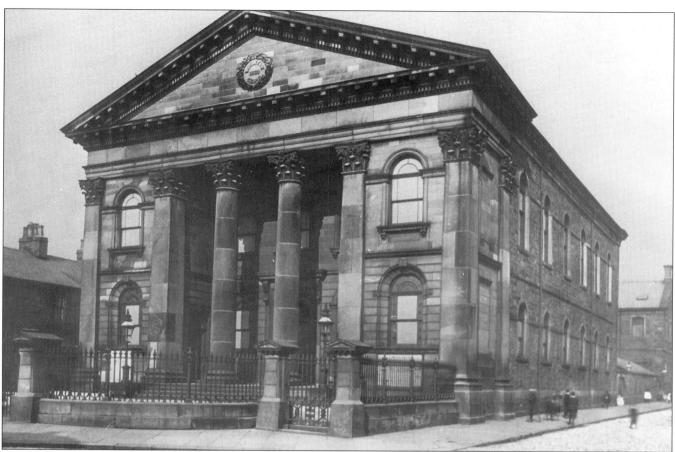

The magnificent frontage of the former Fulledge Wesleyan Chapel in Todmorden Road, which later served several purposes, the last as a kitchen and bathroom showroom, before being destroyed by fire.

In a more modern idiom in the town centre list of churches, Sion Baptist Church occupies a prominent site in Church Street next to Sainsbury's.

Over in Padiham, looking up the hill of the main street in Queen Victoria's time is still a recognisable view today.

A view from a little further back down the street.

Back down the hill to where the new Town Hall was to be built many years later.

These characters are recorded as being local board employees who looked after the gas and water supplies before Padiham had a council.

Surrounding villages have become popular residential areas with new housing estates. In quieter times, this was the leafy scene at Lane Top in Fence.

And this spot by the River Calder at Ightenhill was popular with walkers and picnickers.

An old traction engine can be seen in a lane of old Read village.

Sagar Hill Farm yard scene at Higham in 1905.

Gawthorpe, the stately home of the Shuttleworths, is now owned by the National Trust and attracts many visitors.

Spenser's House at Hurstwood has associations with the poet Spenser.

Huntroyde Hall at Padiham was long the home of the Starkie family.

Palace House in Padiham Road was the former home of the Bishops of Burnley, and is now a nursing home.

The now demolished Bank Hall.

The Holme at Cilviger has also become a nursing home.

Read Hall played host to village events during the days of the Hindley family.

Burnley has more than its share of hotels and pubs, many with historic associations. Right there, almost opposite the churchyard in the oldest part of town and old market square, was the original Sparrow Hawk.

Also in Top of th' Town, only a stone's throw away, was the Talbot.

The new Talbot Hotel, and part of the New Sparrow Hawk on the right.

This was how the Bull and Butcher once looked at the top of Manchester Road.

An early impression of the Bull Inn.

The Bull at the junction of Manchester Road and St James's Street became the town's premier hotel with many important social functions being held there, the building being replaced by Burton's in the 1930s.

The Massey's Burnley Brewery sign is visible on the left of the Cross Keys Hotel at the bottom of Westgate.

The Cross Keys in more recent days.

Early picture of the Black Bull at Lane Head, with a more recent picture inset.

How the Bridge Inn in Bank Parade once looked.

The Commercial Inn at Padiham.

The old Woodman Inn in Todmorden Road, Burnley.

This picture took in three pubs in one go – the Boot Inn, the old White Lion and, on the far right, the Clock Face Inn.

The Hall Inn which was on the corner of Church Street and Hall Street.

The Sun Inn which stood in Bridge Street.

The Duke of York Hotel at the junction of Colne Road and Briercliffe Road, long before it became an 'island' in the present gyratory traffic system.

Whatever the occasion, it was one for being 'dressed up' at the Lane Ends.

The Thorn Hotel was a popular residential inn and watering hole for many local people until it was demolished in the town centre redevelopment of the 1960s.

Opened in 1959 as the luxury four-star flagship hotel of Massey's Burnley Brewery, the Keirby, named after a former brewery once occupying a similar site, has changed hands many times since Massey's closed. Its most recent title is the Comfort Friendly Stop Inn.

The World at Work

Different aspects of the industry when cotton was king in Burnley.

This mill group is unidentified, other than that it was pictured in Burnley.

Note the youngsters in this weaving shed at Perseverance Mill, Hapton – probably half-timers who spent half their day at school and the other half at work.

Again youngsters are in the frame of this scene at O. & J.Folds' Trafalgar Shed.

The faces don't portray much excitement but the bunting above the looms confirm that the occasion was Armistice Day celebrations in 1918 at Lancaster's Mill in Burnley Wood.

Earlier still, this gathering around the looms was at Walton's Mill, Hapton, about 1908.

No date is given for this group of girl workers at Grove Mill.

This group of weavers worked at the George Street Manufacturing Company at Coronation Mill, *c.*1912.

At the time of this picture in the weaving shed of the Harle Syke Mill Company in 1905, there were almost 90 manufacturers in spinning and weaving in Burnley – which lends credence (allowing for slight exaggeration) to the saying that 'you could see 100 mill chimneys in Burnley from above the town at Crown Point' – that is when the smog cleared sufficiently to let you observe the view.

With early morning starts the order of the day in the mills, and the threat of being locked out if you were late, the knocker-up rattling your bedroom window was an essential part of life.

The typical cotton operatives' dress of clogs and shawls for the women and cloth caps for the men (in this case evident at Springhill Mill in Springhill Road) set an image of northerners which has been difficult to live down.

'Pull that barge, tote that bale' – not exactly 'Old Man River', as these workers load the bales at O. & J. Folds' Trafalgar Mill.

Couldn't they have got any more on their lorry? – a load like this would surely be regarded as unsafe today and would attract the attention of the law.

Big mill fires occasionally brought disaster for cotton firms. This blaze was at Byerden Mill (also known as Lodge Mill) in Burnley Lane in October 1905.

This was the aftermath of 'the great fire' at Cooper's at Scar Top.

A more recent celebration by the looms, although the firm is not identified.

The choosing of Cotton Town Queens was as familiar a ritual as the Wakes Weeks at one time. This occasion is not identified.

This picture and the one at the top of the next page of more modern mill times were at Quality Silks, a textile firm which flourished first at Spring Gardens Mill, Colne, and later at Park Shed, Burnley.

Above and left: By the late 1950s, the textile industry was beginning to experience cheap competition from abroad. Short-time working became a feature and into the 1960s firms were beginning to close. King Cotton in Lancashire was dying a slow death with only a tiny handful of firms left today. The felling of the mill chimneys symbolised the end of a great industrial era.

The Burnley coal seams made the mining industry a major one for many years. But in the coal strike of 1921, this picture shows it was a case of 'dig your own coal' at Cheapside.

This pit is unnamed but is described as being 'almost in the town centre and not very noticeable because little waste was dumped'. It was sunk in 1876 and closed in 1953.

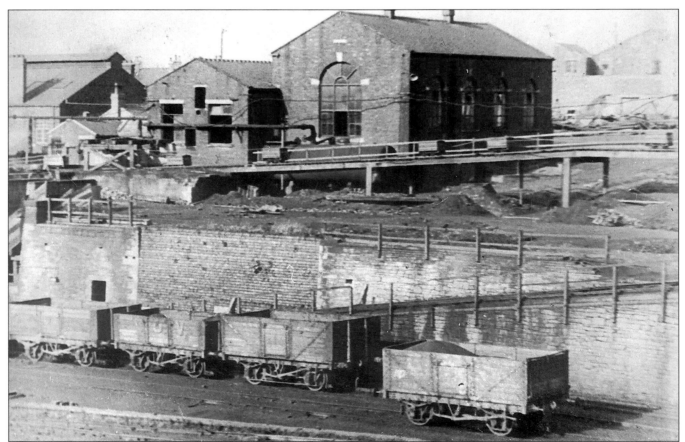

Landscaped parkland with a mining memorial is the legacy on the site of what was Burnley's biggest pit of recent years, Bank Hall, off Colne Road. It was closed in 1971 after it was judged to have become too dangerous to work.

Towneley Pit, one of the many whose winding wheels were once a familiar town sight, along with the gravity-powered 'ginny' train tracks which once fed the coal to the canalside and provided free but dangerous rides for daring youngsters.

These miners were pictured at Hapton Valley Colliery.

Hapton Valley miners voting in a 1974 ballot, resulting in the national coal strike which led to the country experiencing a three-day working week and the downfall of the 1970-74 Heath Government.

This was the tragic scene on 22 March 1962, when an explosion ripped through Hapton Valley pit and caused 19 deaths, a time of mourning for the town and district which exceeded any for any other industrial disaster in living memory. When Hapton Valley closed, it was the end of coal mining in Burnley.

Road and rail transport, Corporation services and hospitals were a major source of employment in good times and bad. This gang were at work on the tram track in Yorkshire Street near the Culvert.

Workers at Massey's Burnley Brewery in Westgate, whose pubs and products were familiar in the town and further afield for many years.

With the loss of Massey's bottling plant on closure of the brewery, drinkers had to go without, among other things, the company's renowned prize pale ale.

Massey's wasn't the only brewery in the area. There was Grimshaw's, and this building housed Cliviger brewery. And today the tradition of brewing in the town is carried on at Moorhouse's, with its noted Premier and Pendle Witch brews.

Soldiers in World War One were supposed to return home to a 'land fit for heroes to live in'. For many, however, the reality was unemployment. Some here, including the disabled, found work at this establishment, and the Towneley Smallholdings were originally intended to provide a home and occupation for returning ex-servicemen.

Besides industries supporting textiles or supplying its workers, a multitude of other businesses of all kinds flourished. This was the rope works at Padiham.

Employees posed for this picture at the Hapton firm of John Riley & Sons.

This group were also
pictured in Hapton, but
their identity is unknown.

It needs only one man to run
a business, and this was Old
Brough (Thomas
Middleborough), the 'dolly blue man'.
The *Express* took this picture to celebrate
his retirement in 1942 as the town's
oldest street hawker. He had held a
pedlar's licence since he was 18 and sold,
among other goods, soap, firelighters,
matches and dolly blue from his
handcart. He retired at 74 'because of this
coupon business' – the issue of wartime
ration books.

Another familiar figure going from door to door at that time was the muffin man, who sold muffins, crumpets and oatcakes from the basket over his arm. The identity of this one is not known.

Burnley factories hummed to the sound of continuous output in the last war, producing anything from munitions and parachutes to aircraft parts. This was the scene on the shop floor at Lupton & Place, a firm still going strong today.

Early transport for circulating the *Burnley Express* to newsagents.

A later transport fleet – in 1955, with the Bull Street *Express* offices decked out for the royal visit.

Assembling the *Express* pages in type – the old hot metal printing process, seen here with workers operating by emergency gas light during a power cut, possibly in the 1974 coal strike.

The computer room at the *Express* after photo-typesetting took over from the old hot metal printing process, an update on communications technology in which investment at the *Express* is still going on today.

The *Express* offices as they look today on the corner of Manchester Road and Bull Street. It is a building which has seen many changes to adapt to ever-advancing technology, although it still incorporates premises which were once part of the old Bull Hotel, including its stables and hay loft.

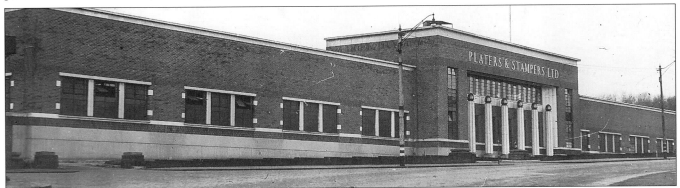

During the unemployment of the early 1930s, Burnley Council took the bold step of building one of the first 'advance' factories. The move paid off handsomely, with production by Platers & Stampers beginning there in 1937. It has been occupied continuously since then, and expanded, with the Prestige Group turning out its famous products there today.

Lucas became among the town's best-known industrial names during the war and afterwards, in its hey day having several factories and thousands of workers in Burnley, turning out aircraft, aerospace and automotive products. The firm had its own sports ground at Reedley and its annual gala there was one of the biggest family events of the year. Skilled sheet metal workers played their part at Lucas in the development of the jet engine and today the firm makes missile casings. This is the firm's Heasandford industrial estate factory.

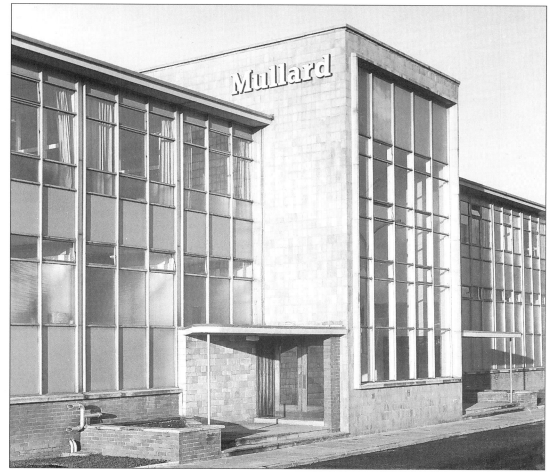

At the time this picture was taken at Padiham's Gothic Works, the firm was known as Glover & Main, and has since seen several name changes, including those of Main-Morley, Main Gas Appliances and Thorn EMI, and today is occupied by Potterton-Myson.

Along with Michelin and Belling, Mullard became one of the new firms which came to the area to boost its industrial success. The firm made TV tubes and built its own glass-making factory, surviving today under the name of Philips Components.

The Market & Shops

Burnley got its Market Charter 700 years ago. The old market place was near the parish church at Top o' th' Town, but this picture of the Market Place/Howe Street is near its present site.

Buildings on the right in the main picture will be more recognisable in the top left inset, which shows a glimpse of the old Empress Hotel on the right.

Architect's drawing of the Market Hall, a building many were to mourn when demolition became part of 1960s development plans.

The market in all its old glory with market-day trading in full swing.

Even today's annual Pot Fair bargains could not compete with John Harrison's indoor market offer in 1896 of a dinner service for six people for ten shillings and sixpence, half a guinea (or 52½p to us).

Another indoor market view as the building neared its final days.

A popular refreshment stall, Hebden & Duxbury's Empire Pea Establishment in Market Street, was demolished in 1934.

The front of the market building with hoardings already heralding demolition work.

Buildings on the market side of St James's Street and the market itself come under the demolition hammer.

First foundations of the new market under construction in 1967. The redevelopment was a joint venture between Burnley Council and the property company, Hammerson's. The building contract went to local firm Howarth Construction Company, which unfortunately encountered unexpected difficulties because of ground conditions and went into liquidation. Work was completed by Costain.

Market traders were able to carry on business in this temporary building until their new first-floor stalls were ready.

And this is how it all looked from Curzon Street when completed, a functional building which didn't suit those who appreciated the architecture of the old premises.

The Market Square as we remembered it until 1995 when the Charter Walk Shopping Centre development altered the picture again.

Burnley's main Co-operative building in Hammerton Street became redundant when the new Pendle (Living) store opened in the Market Square, followed by Leo's (Pioneer) supermarket. Here, the 'to let' signs are already up. Until the Mechanics refurbishment, the Garrick Club amateur theatre productions were staged in this building, and today the shops have a variety of business occupants.

Alfred Cooper's tripe-dressing business also manufactured neatsfoot oil and tallow, had its works in Arch Street, and announced that it supplied shops daily.

Today, you'll find Haffner's butchers' shop, established in 1889, in Keirby Walk, but when this picture was taken the business was in Yorkshire Street.

Poultry and game was hung outside at J.Green's Colne Road fish and fruit business at its Murray Street corner, and express delivery was by pony and cart.

And there was still a fruiterer's shop on the corner of Murray Street when this photograph was taken more recently.

Tin baths and washing
baskets were obviously
big sellers at this shop at
20 Temple Street seen
from Oxford Road.

More outside food displays
at Webster's butchers' shop
in Burnley Road, Padiham, a
well-known business whose
closure in 1989 brought the
end of an era.

A popular emporium in its day, Cheap John's Bazaar at the bottom of Hammerton Street was to give way to Bradley's outfitters (inset, top right).

Marks & Spencer's St James's Street store took on a patriotic appearance for the coronation of Elizabeth II in 1953.

These shops were to disappear from Padiham Road when demolition was needed for the approach to the new roundabout entry to the M65.

Colne Road is still a busy shopping area, which has recently become home to several 'fast food outlets', with some residents complaining about the litter problem.

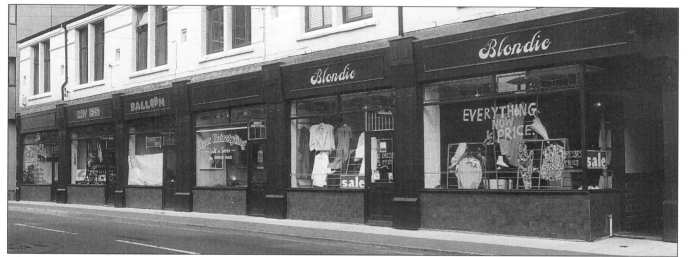

The bottom end of St James's Street has struggled to avoid a faded air, with several businesses doing their best to brighten it up. This fairly recent refurbishment just around the corner in Brown Street made a good attempt.

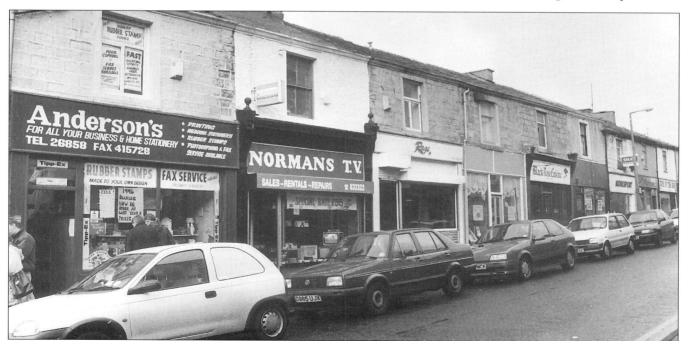

Cut off by the market complex but not forgotten, Standish Street remains a busy shopping area.

Getting Around

P.Eastwood Ltd, coach proprietors, whose premises at the time of this picture were in Manchester Road, was a prominent name in passenger transport from the horse-drawn to cars, taxis and charabancs.

A line-up of Eastwood's horse-drawn vehicles made a fine show.

Keeping their hats on must have presented quite a problem for these ladies in the days of open-air horse-drawn 'coach' outings.

This was Burnley's last 'cabby', Jack Gawoth, of Newcastle Street, pictured about 1936.

This is how Dr H.Chadwick, pictured with his groom, went about his rounds, seen here at the entrance to Towneley Holmes.

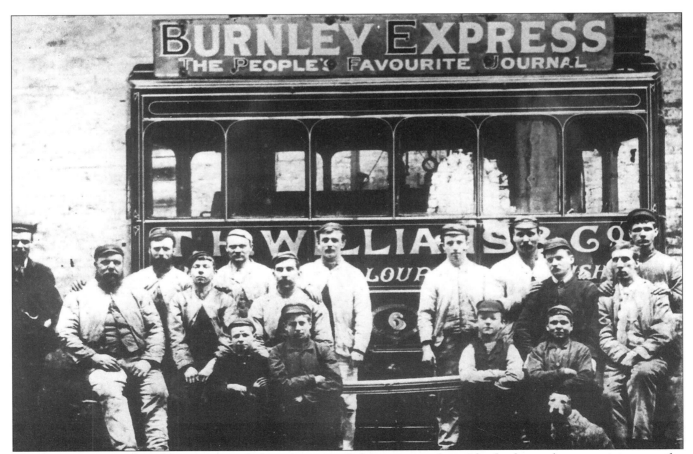

The first step towards public transport before the turn of the century, alongside the horse-drawn variety, was the steam tram, a noisy intrusion on the town's streets. The staff shown here had a doggy mascot – and, from the vehicle pictured it can be seen that the power of advertising was already established.

The coming of the electric tramcar had not overtaken the use of horse power, as this picture at Duke Bar illustrates.

The dangers, as well as the benefits, of improving transport were made evident by this picture of a disaster just before Christmas in 1923 in which two people died. The double-decker tramcar ran away backwards down Briercliffe Road, overturning on the bend at Lane Head. Two tramcars overturned in Colne Road in 1935, but the occupants survived with cuts and bruises.

Already the motor car had made its appearance on the roads, of which this was an early example.

And again it wasn't all travel without tears. This accident was recorded by the camera at Cheapside in 1909.

The destinations of these two outings is unknown, but the vehicle in the picture of the adults' trip is licensed 'to carry 23 people at 12 mph'!

This was the scene at the Parker Lane bus station, the suitcases proclaiming that it was probably the start of the Burnley Fair holiday week.

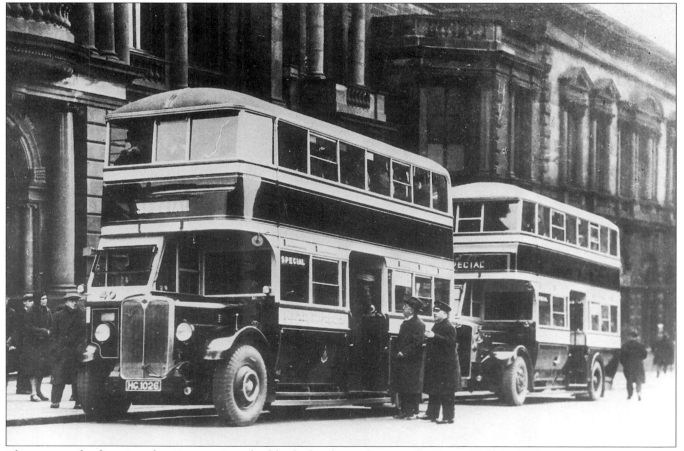

These were the first Burnley Corporation double-decker buses leaving the Town Hall in 1932.

In this picture of St James's Street in 1932, trams and buses were running alongside, but the days of the trams were numbered.

This group of local railwaymen gathered before local passenger services and freight traffic declined.

A pin-up 'clippie' on the Burnley, Colne and Nelson Joint Transport wartime buses.

Locos in a line-up outside the Rosegrove motive power depot.

This Class 8F loco was pictured at Rosegrove on 5 August 1968, in the final days of steam, the Rosegrove depot being one of the last to close.

Rosegrove was always an important junction – this was the old station – and was the terminus of the 'motor train', the 'push-and-pull' which ran a regular to-and-fro service to Colne, with intermediate stops at New Hall Bridge (Burnley), Reedley Hallows and Bott Lane (Colne). The service ceased about 1955.

This was the new Rosegrove station, although seen here in a faded mode in its later days, with some of the once extensive freight marshalling yard tracks in the foreground.

Bank Top was Burnley's main station on the Colne-Preston line.

Following an outcry about the state of Bank Top, British Rail was eventually persuaded to rebuild in the 1960s. The new station, named Burnley Central, had much reduced platform buildings.

Meanwhile, passenger traffic on the line from Gannow junction into Yorkshire declined and eventually ceased, and this became the scene of dereliction at Manchester Road station. Picture by Lynn Millard.

It took the merger of Burnley Building Society with a Bradford counterpart to form the National & Provincial to revitalise the line, with trains being provided to transport Burnley employees to and from Bradford. The line became even more utilised, and today's Manchester Road, pictured here, was reborn.

At one stage, Burnley
Barracks station became the
best-used in the town.

The Leeds and Liverpool Canal
enjoyed a long period of industrial
activity carrying coal and cotton,
with many mills built along its
route. This is the Toll House,
which has become a museum and
a focal point of the restoration
work on the canal stretch in the
Weavers' Triangle.

Many pictures have been taken of the old and new Yorkshire Street canal aqueduct at street level. Here work is in progress at water level – with the water excluded.

Still at the aqueduct, known locally as the Culvert, in September 1925.

This shows cleaning work in progress at the aqueduct in 1954.

This is the canal at Slater Terrace in the Weavers' Triangle, where redevelopment work is in the pipeline.

The famous Burnley 'straight mile' stretch looking from the Finsley Gate end towards the aqueduct and Ormerod Road.

Public Services

Early days of the Burnley Fire Brigade.

The old fire station in Manchester Road was well trimmed up for the coronation of King George V and Queen Mary.

The brigade takes delivery of a gleaming engine with extending ladders.

After many years, the brigade moved its headquarters from Manchester Road to the new station in Belvedere Road, opened in 1965.

The county borough's impressive line-up of fire-fighting vehicles in the Belvedere Road station.

Burnley also had its own police force up to local government reorganisation in 1974. The force was on parade here heading up Manchester Road on Mayor's Day in 1949.

This pre-1914 picture shows work on the construction of Hurstwood reservoir.

These were the men (and one woman) who guided Burnley affairs as the County Borough Council, pictured some time between 1929 and 1931, during the mayoralty of Alderman H.R.Nuttall, JP.

Avid young readers in the children's section of Burnley Central Library. This room later became the lecture hall but, under the latest refurbishment, has reverted to housing the children's library.

Burnley had three swimming pools: this one in North Street, now demolished, the upgraded facilities at Gannow, and Central Baths (also demolished) behind the Town Hall.

Thanks to Burnley benefactor Mr William Thompson, whose fortune was made in the cotton industry, the two old swimming pools were replaced by the Thompson Recreation Centre, and the new Padiham Pool catered for citizens at that end of the borough. For the Burnley project, Mr Thompson originally donated £350,000, matched by a similar amount from the Corporation, for a lido at Thompson Park, which had been given earlier by another member of the family. But the scheme grew into the building of this all-purpose recreation centre.

Mr Thompson did not live to see the opening of the centre, but his sister, Sarah, performed the opening jointly with the 1974 Mayor of Burnley, Councillor Eddie Hanson.

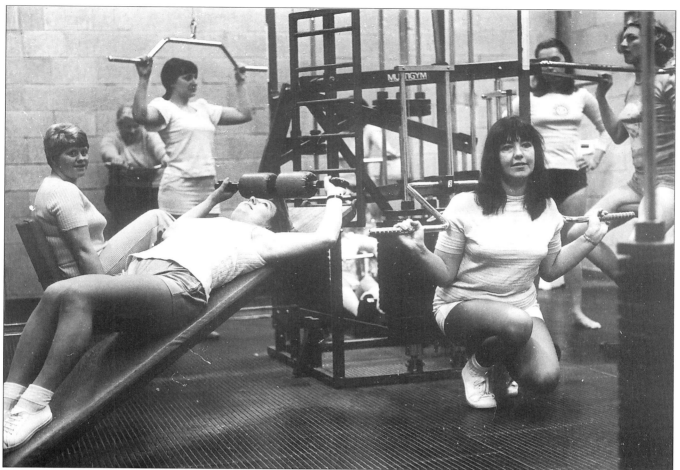

Keeping fit at the well-equipped Thompson Centre.

The jewel in Burnley's crown, Towneley Hall Museum and Art Gallery, probably pictured here in 1937, the flag flying for the coronation of King George the VI and Queen Elizabeth.

The magnificent and classical entrance hall at Towneley.

The view over the park from the hall's battlements as seen in 1965.

Lady Alice Mary O'Hagan, who died in 1921, was the last private owner of Towneley before the Corporation bought the hall and grounds.

Burnley is a town well blessed with parklands. None was more popular in yesteryear on sunny summer days than Thompson Park, with its paddling pool.

Thompson Park again, this time with its boating lake.

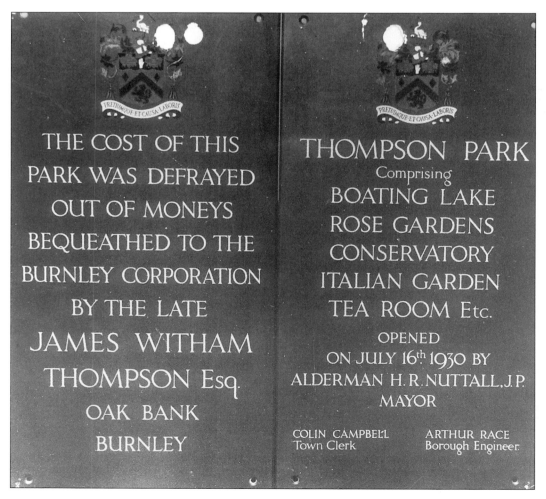

These plaques commemorate the gift by the man who enabled the creation of the park and the opening in 1930.

Queen's Park – a leafy scene in grounds which remain popular with bowlers and tennis players.

Scott Park became somewhat notorious in the controversial Council move to ban dogs from the parks, which attracted national media attention – and resulted in one defiant dog lover going to jail. The park has also suffered at the hands of vandals.

Thursby Gardens opened up a new approach from Colne Road to Bank Top railway station.

Nursery education is not a new issue – here's a scene in Accrington Road nursery of some years ago.

Church schools played an important part in the development of education in Burnley. This was Back Lane School, which was attached to St Matthew's Church.

Gathering of long ago in the wet schoolyard of Coal Clough infants – a picture which the photographer entitled 'After the bell rings'.

These were scholarship winners at Heasandford School in 1913.

The date of this picture of the old Grammar School, now Burnley College's higher education centre, is not certain – probably in the 1940s.

There couldn't be a greater difference between the fine old grammar school building, showing up even better these days after stone cleaning work, and the replacement grammar school of brick and glass, which is now Habergham High School.

Education for the working man was the primary role of the Mechanics' Institutes movement which spread over the country. Burnley Mechanics' building in Manchester Road, as can be seen here, was in being before the next-door Town Hall.

The Technical School and Girls' High School were in these premises, which became Burnley College.

Next page: The old Ormerod Road buildings have grown with extensions at the rear in keeping with Burnley College's changing and expanding role.

The Mechanics has seen many glittering occasions and served many purposes. It has a housed a Mecca dance hall, night club and casino, church institute, and art gallery, and centenary and civic balls have been held there. Once, the roof caved in only hours after the end of a crowded social function.

After years of wondering why the town couldn't boast a decent theatre or civic hall, it was decided to refurbish the Mechanics. Following a feasibility study and much debate, work began on converting the building into an arts and entertainments complex, culminating in the opening by the Queen in 1986.

And eventually it's ready

The Queen opens the new Mechanics in 1986.

Since then many audiences have enjoyed a varied diet of entertainment there – including the now established annual Blues Festival, which has a worldwide reputation – but none more so than youngsters like these, whose needs have been well catered for.

Entertainment and Events

The end for the Cattle Market Gaiety Theatre, as the centre billboard appears to announce the sale of its theatrical effects and furnishings. The date is unclear, possibly 1916.

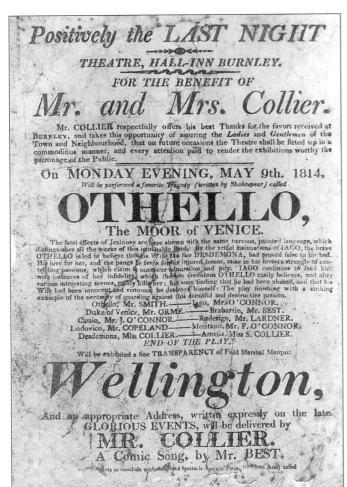

One of the earliest announcements for a theatre production in Burnley. The 'late glorious events' referred to were the taking of Paris, in March 1814, the abdication of Napoleon and his exile to Elba. His return and Waterloo were yet to come.

Dancing and wrestling bears were once popular street entertainment, a scenario that would horrify today's animal activists. This one, suitably muzzled, was performing in Colne Road.

Nowhere was the world of the local stage held in greater affection than Burnley's Victoria Theatre, opened in 1886, which saw the appearance of all the great names of music hall and variety from Charlie Chaplin onwards. Generations of children enjoyed pantomime there and during the war the best of ballet and opera was performed when the theatre became a safe haven from the blitz and headquarters for Sadler's Wells. It was *Hobson's Choice* when closure came in 1955.

And this was the final curtain for the Palace in the town centre. Burnley Light Opera Society performed there from 1958 until 1964, and then moved to the Empire in lower St James's Street, staying there until that closed to live theatre, the final show being *The Sound of Music* in 1970. The Empire carried on as a cinema and later a bingo hall.

The Odeon was the epitome of the luxury cinema with its impressive foyer, staircase and first-floor lounge, all lined with pictures of legendary and glamorous screen star figures.

The big night for the Odeon was the northern premiere in 1961 of the locally-shot film *Whistle Down the Wind*, attended by Mr and Mrs John Mills, star Hayley Mills, producer Richard Attenborough and director Bryan Forbes. Here Hayley arrives with her mother to be presented with flowers and a pair of clogs.

A civic greeting for Hayley Mills from the Mayor and Mayoress of Burnley, Councillor and Mrs Edward Sandy. The audience at the premiere also saw a film about Burnley Football Club, then at the height of fame in the old First Division.

An ignominIous end for the local cinema's flagship as the Odeon is demolished in 1974, leaving a derelict site for some years before the building of the Sainsbury store.

The Savoy Cinema and café also drew the queues for innumerable cinema showings before it, too, bit the demolition dust.

This Stoneyholme cinema had obviously seen better days when this picture was taken.

THE CINEMA, BURNLEY ROAD, BRIERFIELD.

The Management of the above Theatre, request the pleasure of

M ....

... *at the* ...

GRAND OPENING OF THE CINEMA,

on Thursday, July 15th, 1915, at 7-30 p.m.

T. VEEVERS, ESQ., of BRIERFIELD,

will perform the Opening Ceremony.

Entire proceeds devoted to St. John's Ambulance Association and Children's Treat Fund

THIS CARD WILL ADMIT YOU.

This invitation to an opening ceremony at Brierfield was an historic occasion the significance of which would not be fully realised at the time in 1915, for the Burnley Road building today houses Unit 4, the only surviving cinema in the Burnley area. But it has not been a 'continuous' showing. At one period the building served as the 77 Club, with gaming and star cabaret performances, before reopening and being a pioneer of the multi-screen cinema era.

The fire scene at the Empress Ballroom in 1962 was a sad day for thousands who had roller-skated and danced there in the hey-day of the big bands, many of which played their quicksteps, foxtrots and waltzes there and saw many dance floor romances blossom. Another popular dance venue which disappeared, but due to the textile industry's decline and eventual demolition, was the Weavers' Institute in King Street.

Faced with the loss of the Empress, Mecca took over the Mechanics' Institute building to serve as a temporary dance hall, and soon had plans approved for the building of its new Locarno Ballroom on the Keirby roundabout, and which later changed its name to the Cat's Whiskers, finally becoming the Ritzy night club before closure.

This was the gaming scene which, along with star cabaret entertainment, became a feature of night life in the area – at Brierfield, at the Mechanics and at the Cabaret Club in the old cinema building at Rosegrove. It was a revival of live entertainment which wasn't to last all that long.

The discotheque was the new venue for highly-amplified dance music and DJs which were to take over the youth scene. The Angels night spot has been as successful as any in the town, earning fame and attracting fans from over a wide area. This was the opening by the Mayor, Councillor Eddie Hanson, in 1974.

Burnley Fair has always been the big attraction for stay-at-homes during the annual holiday, and this roundabout scene shows one of the big rides in 1906.

And these stalls were thronged with customers about the same period.

The fair has occupied the Cattle Market site, while this one in 1951 set up for business at Hill Top on ground occupied in Church Street today by Sion Baptist Church and Sainsbury's, the present fair venue being Fulledge Recreation Ground.

Burnley has seen many public events and processions up to the present May Day gala days. This carnival was making its way along Padiham Road in the 1920s.

Also in Padiham Road, this shipshape tramcar was dressed overall as HMS Victoria, an idea probably copied from the Blackpool gondola trams, to raise cash for Victoria Hospital.

Church walks had an important place in life in Burnley, and the banners suggest that this gathering near the market was just such an occasion.

Padiham Whit Monday church walks have always been a big occasion: this one was pictured crossing the bridge in 1900.

Nine years later, these walkers were processing along George Lane on Read Walking Day.

This was Rehoboth Church's Walking Day c.1934.

Agricultural shows have had a part to play in local life, even in this predominantly industrial area. This show exhibition had an important statement to make about the town's self-confidence.

Three showground scenes (above and next page) thought to be from the 1948 event.

The busy scene at the Cliviger Show of 1904.

Concert parties were once popular at Sunday school and other organisations' social events. This group formed the Burnley Philharmonic Concert Party, with soprano Elsie Halstead, tenor John Schofield, humorist Jack Sullivan, contralto Rhoda Norman, baritone Harold Jobbins and accompanist Joseph Sharps, and they appeared at Lane Bridge Sunday School in May 1924.

These characters were in Burnley Carnival *c.*1921.

Members of the *Burnley Express* Corner Club had their own concert party, and here's how they looked in 1933.

Both a formal and a pierrot look was chosen by members of the Hapton Church Minstrel Troupe.

Burnley Operatic Society chorus members gathered for this 1936 souvenir picture. The society was the forerunner of the present Burnley Light Opera Society.

This was a Turf Moor football ground appearance by the Rose and Thistle Club Jazz Band and Concert Party.

There was no shortage of Scout troops in Burnley down the years. This group were in camp in Springfield Road in 1944.

Bands have always played a big part in the town's musical heritage. This Scout outfit included some of the original members of the St Andrew's troop.

An early Burnley Salvation Army Band had a plenty of instrumentalists to make a big musical impact.

It looks like a Church Lads' or a Boys' Brigade band, but the inscription on the big drum says 'Lads' Club'.

Briercliffe Prize Brass Band were probably boasting new uniforms for this 1933 picture.

District champions – that was this Burnley Alliance Silver Band in the 1950s.

The *Burnley Express* was still reporting war casualties in June 1945, when wartime leader and Prime Minister Winston Churchill visited Burnley to support the National Liberal candidate, Major H.H.M.Mimes, seen next to the great man here in the car at Turf Moor. 'Winnie' got a rapturous reception from Burnley folk – but the Labour sitting member, Mr W.A.Burke, was the election winner later that year. Also in the picture are National Conservative candidates Richard Fort (Clitheroe) and Lt Harvey Nicholls (Nelson and Colne).

Industrial disputes have featured in the cotton industry, in engineering and, in the 1960s, the building industry was hit by the famous 'tea break' strike. This was a strike scene in 1932, although the purpose of the gathering is not known. The original caption suggests the venue is probably in Colne Road near Duke Bar.

Easily the most successful at elections in Burnley was a product of Welsh mining stock, Dan Jones who, with his wife, Phyllis, and family, came to live in the town when 'our Dan' was chosen as Labour Parliamentary candidate. Quickly becoming accepted as a popular and familiar character and MP, he was known to be always willing to help constituents and fight for the town, its industry and communications. He served for 24 years, fighting seven elections, and gaining a record majority of more than 13,000 in 1966. He retired in 1983 and died two years later.

Youth worker Norman Powell pioneered many youth events in the town, including this Youth Week parade in the late 1950s.

These youth representatives were probably marching out on the same day.

And this youth relay race was won by Sandygate YC.

Far left: This special edition of the *Burnley Express*, the only one ever to appear on a Monday, recorded the biggest disaster ever to affect the area: the holiday week Comet air crash in Spain in July 1970, which killed 40 East Lancashire folk. Among the dead were four members of the Britannia pub soccer team at Padiham and three of their keenest supporters. Many mourned the victims at memorial services in Manchester, Burnley and Padiham. The *Express* was out again on the Tuesday to report the aftermath and give more details of the tragic event which left so many families in mourning.

Sporting Days

'Burnley for the Cup' it says on the side of this lorryload of Burnley fans on their way to the match.

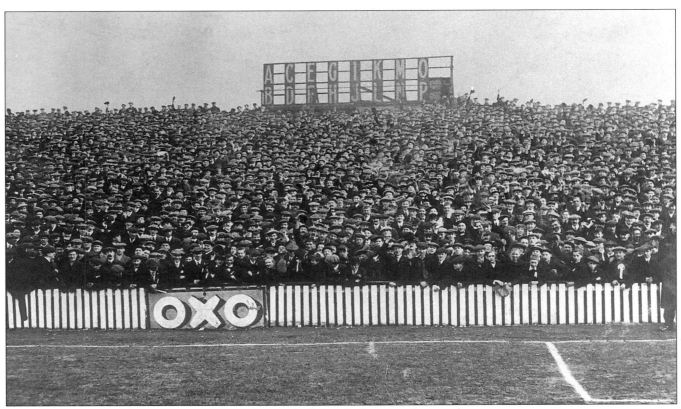

Cloth-capped wearers almost to a man in this packed match day crowd at Turf Moor.

Burnley's 1914 FA Cup-winning squad which beat Liverpool 1-0 at the Crystal Palace.

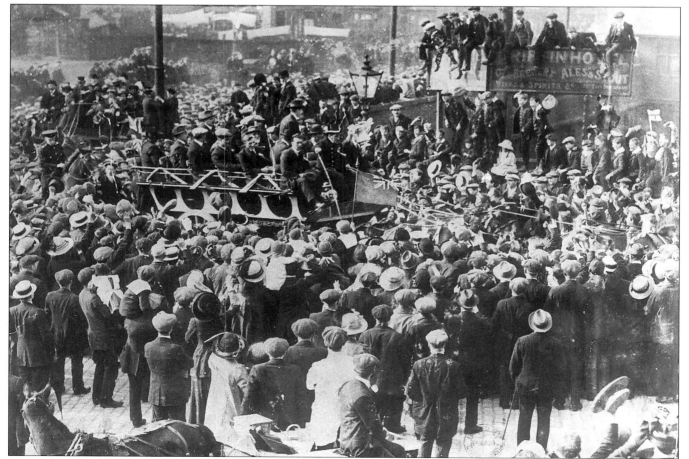

Triumphal return of the 1914 conquering Cup heroes seen here at Rosegrove.

Crowds line the route for the Cup winners.

And this was the greeting outside the Town Hall in Manchester Road.

Legendary player and captain Tommy Boyle poses with the trophy outside the Thorn Hotel in Burnley.

Still the crowds turned out many years later, in 1962 when the Clarets' Cup Finalists returned home, this time without the trophy, having been defeated by old rivals Tottenham Hotspur.

And this was the 1962 Cup squad pictured at Turf Moor before departing for Wembley.

Alan Brown, captain of the 1947 Burnley Cup Final team, presents his side to the Duke of Gloucester at Wembley. The Duke is seen shaking hands with full-back Arthur Woodruff.

An injury victim at Turf Moor in 1953 when a wall collapsed during a match against Sunderland.

Burnley FC manager during the great 1960s era, Harry Potts, is seen here being greeted by club president James Grimshaw.

1960 First Division champions Burnley pose with the trophy.

'We are the champions' – captain Jimmy Adamson raises his glass with the Mayor, Councillor Miss Edith Utley, at the 1960 Town Hall celebrations.

Also enjoying a toast with the Mayor is Bob Lord (left), the football club chairman who was ebullient, outspoken and often the centre of controversy, particularly following the sudden sale of Clarets idol of the 1950s and early 1960s, Jimmy McIlroy.

Burnley were to go on to hit the big time with appearances in European competitions. Here the board and players are pictured 'going continental'.

No game abroad was more sensational than the return Inter-Cities' Fairs Cup match in Naples, which ended in a riot. This was the scramble to get track-suited goalkeeper Adam Blacklaw, who didn't play in the game, to the safety of the dressing-room.

Burnley FC chairman Bob Lord persuaded one of his heroes, Field Marshal Viscount Montgomery of Alamein, to visit Turf Moor in 1967. Here 'Monty' shakes hands with full-back John Angus, introduced by skipper Alec Elder (partially hidden), with Mr Lord and the Mayor, Alderman George Hollinrake, in the background.

Hearty laughter on the occasion of the opening of the Bob Lord Stand at Turf Moor by former Prime Minister Mr Edward Heath in September 1974.

Up-to-date development at Turf Moor with Bertie Bee and mascot Adam Hope, seen on the opening night of the new North Stand on 23 April 1996.

Amateur football from youngsters upwards has also flourished in Burnley, with the Hospital Cup being a keenly-contested competition. This side were Schoolboys' Cup winners in 1935.

Lancashire League Cricket has featured almost all the legendary names in Test cricket among its club professionals. Names like Constantine, Martindale, Weekes, Gilchrist, Lindwall and Dooland spring to mind, just to name a few. But none came to serve at Turf Moor with a bigger and more fearsome reputation than West Indian fast bowler Charlie Griffith. His first search on coming to the town was for a bed big enough to accommodate him. He was professional in 1964 and 1967. In his first season, he took a record 144 wickets.

Cricket at Turf Moor has seen many big occasions and nail-biting finishes over the years, with the match in progress here, in *c.*1901, featuring Burnley Cricket Club playing no less a side than the Australians.

This was the Burnley CC side of 1974, when the professional was an Englishman, Peter Plummer of Nottinghamshlre (front left).

In 1973, West Indian Duncan Carter was the professional at Lowerhouse with this side which ended the season in the lower reaches of the league table.

Padiham Cricket Club has had its days of triumph, and this side were league champions in 1908.

Running is an ancient sport – many were the wagers in the earlier days when some made a living out of it. Today, running is a popular pursuit for fun, fitness and fund-raising, from short-distance events to the marathon stretch. This was the start of a Burnley May Day fun run.

Swimming galas and life-saving classes from school to club level have been popular at local pools. This team, proudly showing off its trophies, was from Massey's Brewery, who were Burton Cup winners in 1939.

Crown green bowling boasts a large following in local leagues for men and women. These matches were in progress at Towneley Bowling Club.

A real Burnley bulldog of boxing! The sport has had many Burnley devotees down the years, from the days of the old fairground booths. Today's leading exponent of the art here is Warren Stowe, who burst on to the professional scene in 1991. He won the Central Area middleweight title and fought for the World Boxing Organisation Penta-continental middleweight championship, losing on points.

Healing the Sick

Said to have been the first isolation hospital, these converted cottages in Briercliffe Road are now demolished. They were opposite the Burnley Workhouse and the unit opened in 1876 to deal with a smallpox epidemic.

There was also said to be an isolation hospital at Crown Point, but this sanatorium dealt with cases needing isolation in later years and, when it closed, what had become known as Marsden Hospital was dealing with chest cases. Its work was transferred to Burnley General Hospital.

Marsden Hospital housed the area's first Hospice Day-Care Centre, but vandals began to plague the site, and this was the demolition scene recently as the grounds made way for a new housing development.

Poverty and old age meant the workhouse for many and these scenes *c.*1900 at the Burnley Union Workhouse on the site of the General Hospital showed the old mangle, the laundry, the sewing department and the dining room.

In the post-war development of the National Health Service, plans for a district hospital on the Burnley General Hospital's Briercliffe Road/Casterton Avenue site went ahead over the years, though there were strong protests at the closures of the Colne, Nelson and Burnley Maternity Hospitals, Hartley Hospital at Colne and Reedyford Hospital at Nelson. Building work under way here at the General Hospital was of a new accident and emergency and out-patients' departments.

Here the General Hospital has acquired the multi-storey Edith Watson Maternity Unit, with the casualty and out-patients' department, front right. It is pictured before the building of the Wilson Hey wards at the back, right.

Victoria Hospital in Thursby Road won the affection of local people over the years, and there was dismay, protests and anger at the sudden closure, after many rumours and denials, at a time money was being raised for its centenary appeal. Here is the stone-laying ceremony in 1884.

Commemorating the occasion of the stone-laying.

An old picture of Victoria Hospital with its circular wards, which were designed to save work, but nursing staff found them confusing and disorientating. The town's accident and emergency department was housed at Victoria until a new unit was built at the General Hospital.

The Edith Watson Maternity Unit at the General Hospital was named after the long-serving chairman of the old Burnley Hospital Management Committee, who is pictured here outside Buckingham Palace with her son and grandson after receiving the OBE. She died in 1963.

Burnley hospital staff, but the date of this picture is not known.

This staff group was pictured during the mayoralty of Alderman and Mrs Ronald Bushby in 1946-47.

Left: Colonel Gladys Cocking, who trained as a nurse at Burnley Victoria Hospital, went on to become second-in-command of the Army Nursing Corps.

These nurses assembled at the Nurse Training School at Reedley on prize-giving day in 1962.

Royal Occasions

The royal visitor on this occasion, in September 1905, was Princess Louise, the Princess Royal, daughter of King Edward VII and Queen Alexandra.

How Burnley folk gathered to hear King George V broadcast a speech to the nation on 23 April 1924.

In May 1938, it was a case of three cheers with hats raised for King George VI and Queen Elizabeth outside the Platers and Stampers factory in Colne Road.

And King George was in RAF uniform to sign in, while the Queen looks on, during their March 1945 visit.

The 1955 royal visit to North-East Lancashire towns, included a Burnley stop when Queen Elizabeth II and Prince Philip were welcomed by the Mayor and Mayoress, Alderman and Mrs Joseph Herbert. On the left is town clerk, Mr C.V.Thornley.

In 1968, the Queen came to Burnley to study the results of Operation Springclean in which efforts had been made to spruce up buildings with a stone-cleaning blitz, and the centre for the visit was St Peter's Parish Churchyard, where there had also been a big improvement scheme. She is seen with Lord Derby, being greeted by the Mayor of Burnley, Alderman John H.Sutcliffe.

The Bishop of Burnley, the Rt Revd G.E.Holderness, smilingly watches the Queen sign the visitors' book.

The Queen meets locals and is seen chatting here to young people.

Passing through the crowd in the churchyard.

In 1986, Prince Charles was in town to visit Queen Street Mill, and to take a look round the Weavers' Triangle, and here, appropriately for a Prince of Wales, he receives a bunch of daffodils.

Prince Charles on the way up Manchester Road towards the canal.

This was the scene at the canal Toll House Museum on the tour of the Weavers' Triangle.

Time to stop to greet many well-wishers along the route.

Prince Charles was accompanied by Princess Diana on the 1986 visit, arriving at Rosegrove Station, but while the Prince toured Burnley, the Princess went on to engagements in Blackburn.

The next six picures represent some of the celebrations in Burnley which greeted Royal Occasions.

Procession time in the main street to mark the Queen's Silver Jubilee celebrations in 1977.

Enthusiastic flag-wavers ready to greet Prince Charles in 1986.

Children out in force to give Prince Charles a Burnley welcome like he's never had before during his visit.

Wartime Days

Second-Lieutenant Victor Smith and Private Thomas Whitham were World War One Burnley holders of the Victoria Cross, but probably Burnley's most famous 'adopted' soldier was General Sir James Yorke Scarlett. He led the charge of the Heavy Brigade at Balaclava in the Crimean War, doing much to save the day after the disaster of the more famous charge of the Light Brigade. But the general lost the day when he stood for election in Burnley, having settled down in the town, living at Bank Hall with his wife, Charlotte Anne, daughter of local coal owner Colonel John Hargreaves. He was noted for his generosity to the poor, particularly during the Cotton Famine.

Evidence of Burnley as a garrison town was to be found in the old barracks buildings between Padiham Road and Barracks Road. This artillery group are seen at the now-demolished barracks in 1915.

The location of this World War One tank, marked '250,000 Burnley', and what was the occasion, are not certain. But, with a couple of tram conductors on the left, tram tracks and overhead wires in view, could it have been at Queensgate?

The battalion assembled here in Burnley during World War One are seen learning field first-aid.

This Burnley Royal Field Artillery contingent is seen in Manchester Road, near the Rose and Crown Hotel.

Old 'vets' members of the 5th Battalion, East Lancashire National Reserve Brass Band.

Fund-raising went on in World War Two, during savings weeks for warships, weapons and to buy a Spitfire. This Burnley Spitfire was made by Abel Street schoolboys under the direction of crafts teacher and renowned local film-maker Mr Sam Hanna.

Dressed as 'Young Kitchener', Jennie Jackson, later Mrs Jennie Flynn, and now aged 88, spent Saturdays during World War One in the town centre collecting money for cigarettes and other comforts for the troops, raising an estimated £4,000, plus another £1,000 for a motor ambulance.

A Padiham Town Hall display invites donations for War Weapons Week, with £40,000 showing on the indicator board.

Mr Sam Hanna was also official photographer for 'Dads' Army', the local Home Guard, seen here on parade.

The Home Guard again, this time aboard a tracked vehicle at the corner of Padiham Road and Park Lane.

The ARP (Air Raid Precautions) men and women, among other duties, patrolled the streets to make sure no lights were showing in the black-out. This was Burnley Wood's ARP 'F' Group in 1940.

This group is not identified. The men are standing in front of a building with a sand-bag covered window, and could have been ARP, auxiliary firemen or ambulancemen.

And this time the lads appear to be in camp, location not known.

Not quite TV's Corporal Jones' butcher's van, but this Home Guard exercise in Padiham had 'commandeered' a civvy vehicle which appears to pack mortar firepower.

The Home Guard band was so successful that it continued after the war, and here its members are seen leading Holy Trinity Church procession in 1950.

ARP workers could rely on mobile canteens for refreshments.

And these ambulances, lined up at Queensgate, look ready to cope with any emergency.

Air-raid shelters sprang up everywhere, at schools, in parks, on spare ground and in the streets. This one was in Thorn Street.